Beavers, Foxes and Grizzly Bears ... Oh, and Cheetahs, Fish and Sloths Too

A Book About Animals, People and Behavior in the Workplace

by

Lawrence Carey and Debra Warner, Psy.D.

Published by Dr. Debra Publishing

Dr. Debra Publishing
ISBN 978-0-578-71953-5
       978-0-578-71954-2

Printed in the United States
1st Printing 2020

ATTENTION: ORGANIZATIONS & CORPORATIONS
Bulk quantity discounts for reselling, gifts or fundraising are available. For more information, please contact letslistenletslove@gmail.com

Cover Design and Illustrations: Dave Warner
Story Arc: Robert Carey, Psy.D.

Dedication

To every kid with a dream.

Acknowledgments

We both acknowledge all who supported us in this process and put in much effort to see it to the end! Lawrence and Mama thank you so much!

A special thank you to Robert Carey, Psy.D. (Daddy) for loving us!

From Lawrence Carey

This book represents a fun process with my Mama. It shows how you can get something done. It also includes my favorite things: animals.

From Debra Warner, Psy.D.

This book represents my relationship with one of the best humans in the world: my son. This book is the love and admiration I have for him and his mind. He can do and be anything. How blessed am I. Thank you, Lord; Thank you.

Table of Contents

Preface

The Importance of This Book

According to Lawrence
This book is about work management and the types of people who work at different places. It's about rank, and how people behave and interact in a social context. If you read this book, you will learn people facts and animal facts and how, by applying that to organizational culture, you can figure out why people do the things they do. We classify people as beavers, foxes, grizzly bears, fish, sloths, and cheetahs. There are other animal groups also, but these are the primary ones we focused on because they are the most prevalent ones in the workplace.

According to Mama (Debra Warner, Psy.D.)
This book came from an idea I had over 15 years ago. I never thought at the time that my 9-year-old son would finish it. This book is important because it teaches about more than organizations. It also shows how to complete a dream and have others support you.

Foreword

Laying the Foundation

Julia Locklear
Ph.D. Candidate, Business Psychology
Los Angeles-based Career Coach and Columnist

Between the time that I was asked to write this introduction and when I submitted it, the world became a very scary place. People are getting sick and we don't have medicine to help them get better. People of color are falling ill and dying at a rate much higher than everyone else. One reason why this is the case is because when things are normal, people of color can't always afford to see a doctor, even if they are sick. Sometimes, even if they do go to a doctor or hospital, the doctors and nurses may not take very good care of them. This makes them less healthy, which means when these people catch COVID-19, it is too much for their bodies to handle.

You also may have seen on the news that people all over the world are protesting against racism. Specifically, they want the police to start treating people of color with dignity and respect, like they do with white people. Most protests have been peaceful, but some have turned into riots with people looting stores and setting restaurants and gas stations on fire. What's even worse is that the police, who are supposed to protect the community, are attacking the peaceful protesters, which is the very behavior they are protesting. While people are scared and sick and don't know when they will be able to leave their houses and travel again, organizational leaders have had to guide their teams with compassion and confidence at a time when the only news seems to be bad news.

So, what is organizational psychology? Organizational psychology is the study of how people behave in the workplace. The roles, customs, and structures that are created by people in the workplace (employees) all come together to create the organizational culture. Healthy organizational cultures, where people work together and are supportive of one another, where leaders are transparent and compassionate, produce positive outcomes. Companies with healthy cultures serve their customers better, make more money, and hang onto their employees. Unhealthy or toxic workplaces produce negative results. Employees stuck in toxic organizational cultures often have a hard time getting out of them. The longer employees remain in toxic cultures, the greater the damage to them personally.

How can you tell if a particular culture is toxic? Oftentimes in an organization with a toxic culture, leaders motivate their employees through fear: fear of being punished for sharing their opinions, fear of hitting a dead-end where they can't advance any further, and fear of losing their jobs. If that sounds like bullying behavior to you, you're right. Some leaders in toxic, and even relatively healthy cultures, are allowed to be bullies either because the organization values the results they achieve over their attitude and treatment of others, or because the organization is afraid to act to stop bullying behavior.

We are also part of a larger organization with a very toxic environment: The United States of America. Our elected officials are like middle management in a corporation. They have some power and are supposed to act in the best interests of the people who elected them but the

CEO of the United States is himself a bully who shows preferential treatment to white employees but makes things harder for employees who are people of color. Fed up with this unhealthy culture, the country is demanding fair treatment for all people.

We also belong to the global community and our coworkers in other countries are protesting racism and unequal treatment in their own communities, as well as to show solidarity with people of color in this country who have had enough.

As I write this, I wonder how a 9-year-old child sees what is going on around him. In the span of just a few months, he had to make sense of a new reality and unsettling events. Then I realized he likely had an organization to reference: His own family. Organizations are systems not unlike families, where everyone plays a role and all parts of the system have to function well, otherwise the work does not get done. Sometimes one or both parents may be president or CEO of the family when it comes to making decisions. There are leaders who function like our mommies and daddies. They tell us what to do, try to teach us new things, and punish us when we do the wrong thing and get into trouble.

Parents try to shape and mold their children into the kind of people they want them to be just like professors and mentors try to help students and employees figure out what they want to be when they grow up. Some employees, as with kids, knew at a very young age what they wanted to be when they grew up. Others may try a few different jobs before deciding what they want to do for a living. Some people never decide. They just go where life takes them and that's enough for them.

Our coworkers are sometimes like our brothers, sisters and even our cousins. We may argue and disagree about who should do which tasks, like household chores, but in the end, we have to work together to get everything done. And just like with siblings and cousins, coworkers don't always get along every day. Sometimes, disagreements are small and maybe someone's feelings get hurt for a little while but eventually, everyone makes up and gets back to having fun and enjoying each other's company.

Some parents are strict, just like bosses. Others want to be your friend, but they might not give you the right guidance about your job, which is, in this case, your life. Some kids receive a bigger allowance than others, just like adults are paid different salaries for different types of work. Sometimes daughters are paid less than sons for doing the same chores. Occasionally, employees are rewarded for hard work or going above and beyond, but there are parents who choose not to reward their children for doing the things they are supposed to do anyway.

In my career I changed jobs fairly frequently to remove myself from toxic cultures. I sometimes reflect on my parents working 12 to 14-hour days in unsupportive environments to gain a promotion or better job fit. I think about how as a child I learned about organizational culture. In this book, Lawrence, in his 9-year-old wisdom, is piecing together what he views as organizational issues and relating them to his knowledge base. He uses animals and his childlike database to break down hard issues in a refreshing narrative story. You could replace the animal characters with many different people in an organization and see the issues clearly.

This book explains organizational structure, obligations and employee struggles while providing a clear definition of the problems and solutions. It can assist many organizations in today's climate of uncertainty. Please take in the content as you read and think about how you can apply the information.

Section I: Providing a Framework

Chapter 1

Narrative Structure

This book will explain organizational culture through the framework of a narrative story using animals throughout. In this chapter, are all the animal characters. Characters are to be seen with humanistic qualities. They are described as Lawrence sees them and how they fit into an organization due to their behavioral qualities for purposes of this book.

Beavers
Behavior

Beavers are nocturnal. They are busy each night building and mending their habitats. Beavers work year-round but are less active in cold. They are "nature's engineers." They are social and peaceful and like to work as a collective. They are territorial but do not attack unless provoked.

Behavior in an Organization

Beavers are organized, managers. They can put things together and be in charge. They are administrators or owners of a business. They are also subordinates that can follow people in charge. They can attain higher ranks, but they will always be beavers. They will always act the same. They will never change depending on rank. They fit best in middle management.

Narrative Story Character

Billy Beaver, Team Leader

Billy Beaver is a manager who wants to be successful. He is a hard worker and completes all his engineering tasks with his team. He is getting promoted to administration. He does not want to take the promotion. He wants to stay and work with his team. He has managed this team for 10 years and feels his coworkers are like family.

Foxes

Behavior

  Foxes are also nocturnal. They prefer to hunt and work alone. They are not pack animals. They can be discreet when hunting and plan activities. They have high reasoning ability and find ways to outsmart traps and hunters.

Behavior in an Organization

  Foxes are manipulative and work alone. They try to get ahead but don't get anywhere. They tend to be shady. They can be in leadership but usually it does not work because they are self-oriented and do not understand team interactions. They try to influence people in a manipulative way. They also create loopholes that give them all the credit. Foxes can answer to beavers but they're always striving to get ahead.

Narrative Story Character

  Freddy Fox, Beaver Team 1

  Freddy Fox also known by the nickname "Sly." He does not think of himself as shady. He wants a promotion for himself and does not care about his teammates. He has a history of complaints regarding sabotage that no one can prove.

Grizzly Bears

Behavior

Grizzly bears are solitary animals but will be with others when resources are abundant. They are strong, but do not defend their territory unless they feel threatened. Others respect grizzlies due to their size and the possibility of being hurt in an attack.

Behavior in an Organization

Grizzly bears are in charge of the company. The top leaders are seen as such due to their solitary nature and large presence. They are bosses, the CEOs. They answer to a board of directors (lions). They are the ones who oversee interactions in the department and make sure resources are distributed appropriately and abundantly for use.

Narrative Story Character

Benny Bear, President of Project Implementation

Benny Bear wants to promote Billy Beaver. He believes everyone can be better, but he does not like manipulators like Freddy Fox.

Sloths

Behavior

Sloths move slowly so that they use the least amount of energy to get through the day. It is a survival technique and part of their metabolic needs. They are precise in their movements.

Behavior in an Organization

They are the slow ones. They don't get much work done because they are going so slowly. But what is done is done well when it's finished. They probably do the best work when they finish on time. Being speedy does not work for the sloth. They are focused on what is needed for the task.

Narrative Story Character

Sonya Sloth, Administrative Assistant to Billy Beaver Sonya Sloth works really slowly and barely gets anything done. When she does get it done, she does it very well. She does what should she do and no more. She needs training to work faster. If not, she will not get promoted due to how slow she is. She knows Billy Beaver values her but wonders if her next boss will do the same.

Fish

Behavior

Fish have collective behavior and intelligence. They act and respond together for survival and will often hide from threats and move together for safety and protection.

Behavior in an Organization

Fish work in groups. They get their work done together and are good workers. While others work outside of their group, most fish just stay within the group. They work together as a team. They are not independent workers. They may not be able to get along with new team members and that causes new members to leave the group. Fish can be problematic to manage. Fish need other fishes to be productive. Most schools have 5 to 7 members, 8 is unlikely.

Narrative Story Characters

Franky, Freeda, Felix, Fernando, and Phil Beaver Team 1The fish are your normal employees who work together to get the job done. Since Billy Beaver is to get the manager promotion, they were asked to join him, but they are trying to think of the benefit for their school and if supporting Billy Beaver will help them.

Cheetahs

Behavior

Cheetahs are the fastest land animals in the world. They are skilled hunters and have a good sense of balance. They interact mainly in small groups or alone.

Behavior in the Organization

Cheetahs are the ones that want to get everything done and go home. Their fast work means they can be disorganized as they try to get everything done quickly to get paid and go home. Cheetahs don't care about their coworkers. Their work is sloppy. These behaviors interfere with their relationships with others.

Narrative Story Character

Chandler, Chelsea, and Chuck

Beaver Team 1

The cheetahs do not want Billy Beaver to get the promotion because Billy Beaver is set in his ways and does not believe in going home early. He thinks there is always work to be done. The cheetahs want to get done and go home. Billy Beaver wonders if he should let go of his beliefs.

Lions

Behavior

Lions work together and are patient. They try to understand and size up the situation to make calculated decisions that are best for group survival.

Behavior in an Organization

They are the chairman of the board, the king of the organization. They are in charge of ensuring the organization runs smoothly, that finances are in place. The board looks at profits and losses and ensures the company is sound. Lions usually only interact with leadership. They do not interact with cheetahs, fish or other subordinates unless it affects the whole business.

Narrative Story Characters

Leo, Leah, Lawrence, Leanna and Leopold
Board of Directors

The lions all think that new leaders should have certain qualifications. Half think Billy Beaver should be put in management, the other half are against it. Chairman Lawrence has to decide what is best for the company.

Cougars

Behavior

Cougars travel in small family packs until mature enough to leave and make their own family pack. They are social with each other and keen in survival in harsh conditions.

Behavior in the Organization

Their concern is for their family needs. Cougars share both cheetah and sloth traits. Half of them want to get work done to go home, but their work is both sloppy and good. They are in-between. They just exist. They do not take responsibility and will often give responsibility to others to avoid making mistakes. Their goal is to have a job in order to survive and support their family. The type of job does not matter. They are just interested in maintaining the status quo.

Narrative Story Characters

Caitlin and Clive Cougar

Beaver Team 1

The cougars have no opinion about the manager promotion. They only care about keeping their jobs. They will take any side that keeps their positions intact. They have no feelings about others but are only concerned about supporting their families.

Backwoods Builders LLC

Lawrence Lion
Chairman
Board of Directors
And an all-around great guy

The Lions
Board of Directors

Benny Bear
VP Project Implementation

Billy Beaver
Team Leader

Freddy Fox
Special Assistant to Billy Beaver
(or so he thinks)
Assigned to Beaver Team 1

Sonya Sloth
Administrative Assistant to Billy Beaver
Assigned to Beaver Team 1

Cheetahs
Chandler, Chelsea, and Chuck
Assigned to Beaver Team 1

Cougars
Caitlin and Clive
Assigned to Beaver Team 1

Fish
The Fabulous Five
Franky, Freeda, Felix, Fernanda, and Phil
Assigned to Beaver Team 1

Organizational Structure

Section II: The Story

Chapter 2

Backwoods Builders: A Lawrence Laing Company

Robert Carey, Psy.D.

This story illustrates the theory of Binary Responsibility and how it can manifest in the workplace using animals in various job roles.

Benny Bear shifted in his seat, nervously waiting for his chance to speak. The grizzly bears rarely met in person so when a meeting was called to discuss "important things," Benny feared this could mean big trouble.

Betty Bear, the CEO, drummed her claws on the table, as was her habit when she was deep in thought. Betty was a mama bear and Backwoods Builders was her baby. If something threatened the organization, she would do anything to protect it, even if it meant firing bears. Finally, she broke her silence.

"If the dam is not finished by spring, there won't be enough fish in the lake, and the board will not be pleased. I certainly don't plan to sacrifice myself and I would rather not have to throw any of you to the lions, either. But we need a solution here, bears."

All eyes turned to Benny. As vice president of project implementation, it was his responsibility more than anyone else's to make sure the dam was ready in time. His stomach tossed and turned, like that time when he accidentally ate bad berries, but he stood up, smiled broadly, and confidently said, "Don't worry about a thing, boss. I've got my best beaver on the job. He's never let us down before, and I know he'll come through for us this time."

There was a long pause, but Benny didn't waver. He just kept grinning confidently.

"Excellent!" Betty Bear exclaimed.

A sigh of relief arose from the other bears in the room, followed quickly by a chorus of "Good job!" "Great plan!" and "Way to go, Benny!"

Later that day, as the sun began to set, Benny foraged for berries while he waited for Billy Beaver to emerge from his den. Little did Benny know that he was not the only one who wanted to speak to the beaver.

At that moment, Freddy Fox was sauntering through the woods and as he did, he strolled right through Sonya Sloth's garden. She would be furious that he stomped all over her sunflowers, though it would take her a while to react. Of course, Freddy didn't even notice the damage that he did. He was busy cooking up another one of his schemes to get more pay for less work. Soon he was approaching Billy Beaver's den. He was just in time to eavesdrop on Billy and Benny.

"Billy, my old friend, I've got some great news."

"Really, Benny? What is it?"

"Backwoods Builders has won a big contract. We're going to build the biggest dam the woods have ever seen. The timetable is pretty tight and there's a lot riding on this, so I told the boss there is only one beaver I trust to make this happen and that's Billy. Bottom line buddy, you're getting a big promotion."

"Wow! That sounds great! I can't wait to tell the team that we're getting a promotion."

"Billy, we can't put the whole team on this project. The dam is going to be on the other side of the lake, and we need the rest of your team to maintain the dams here. Besides, you won't be on a beaver team anymore. You'll be in charge of all of the north side beaver teams. This is an executive position."

"Not on a beaver team? But I'm a beaver. How can I get all my work done without my team?"

"You'll be fine, Billy. Just look at me. I have an executive position, and you don't see a bunch of other bears following me around, do you?"

"But Benny, you're a bear and you work like a bear. I'm a beaver. I don't know if I can work like a bear."

"I have faith in you, Billy. The company really needs you. Plus, think of how great it will be for your family. You'll get a big raise and the company owns a beautiful beaver den just minutes from your new office. It's yours for free if you'd like."

"I don't know, Benny. It sounds like an awfully big change. Can I take some time to think about it?"

"I've got an even better idea. Instead of just thinking about it, you can try it out and see if you like it. We'll make you the *acting* director of the North Shore Dam Project. You can start Monday, try it out for a few weeks and if it doesn't work out, you can always come back to your old job here. But I'm sure you're going to love it, and I know you'll be great at it. I can't tell you how much the company is counting on you, Billy. Meet me in my office first thing Monday morning and we'll get you started."

At that moment, Freddy Fox stepped out from behind a fir tree.

"Mr. Bear! What a pleasant surprise. I was just on my way to tell the boss here…Good evening, boss…I was just on my way to brief the boss on all the important projects we've got cooking at the old woodshed. We handle our most important projects at the woodshed, but I'm sure I don't have to tell *you* that, sir."

"No. Of course not, um…Fox, right?"

"That's right sir, Freddy Fox, at your service, loyal company employee for the past ten years, Billy Beaver's right hand and if you don't mind me saying so, your biggest fan, sir. Been keeping a close on things at the woodshed for the boss here, but I'm sure I don't have to tell *you* that, sir."

"No, of course not. Mr. Beaver always speaks very highly of you. The old woodshed, that's out behind the hen house, isn't it, Fox?"

"Yes, sir. It is. Nothing gets past you. You are a sharp one, sir."

"Well, I should let you two get to your briefing. Billy, I'll see you Monday. Nice to see you again, um…Fox."

And with that Benny Bear bounded into the backwoods leaving Billy Beaver to listen to Freddy Fox bluster on and on about bodacious benefits and binary something or other. In truth, Billy wasn't listening at all. Freddy never had anything important to say and nothing important ever happened at the woodshed. Billy only gave Freddy an office there to keep him out of the way.

At that moment Billy was feeling rather overwhelmed. He wanted to help the company and he'd love to be able to give his family more of the things they wanted but this new job just didn't sound like the proper sort of thing for a beaver. How could he tell the rest of his team that he was leaving them? It all weighed heavily on his bewildered, beaver brain.

At the end of the worknight, Benny brought the team together as he usually did, to thank them for a good night's work and to iron out plans for tomorrow. As usual, the cheetahs, Chandler, Chelsea, and Chuck, were chomping at the bit to get out and go home. But the conscientious cougars, Caitlin and Clive, cried, "Calm yourselves, cats. We're not ready to roam."

Steady Sonya Sloth simply sat in her seat, secretly seething with scorn, knowing full well Freddy Fox had forgotten how he trampled her tulips, mashed up her marigolds and laid waste to her waterlilies. Finally, the Fabulous Fish Five, Franky, Freeda, Felix, Fernando, and Phil, floated freely about feeling fulfilled. Billy was just about to wrap things up when Freddy suddenly chimed in.

"So, boss, any news from headquarters?"

"Oh, well, um…"

Suddenly, Billy remembered that Freddy had seen him talking to Benny Bear. Billy wasn't really ready to tell the team about his promotion, but he didn't want to lie to them. Freddy's question had sort of put him in an awkward position.

"Well, you see…it's not exactly news really, although I guess you could call it news if you really wanted to, but I certainly don't want to. I would rather think of it as something that might turn into news someday but probably won't because it really doesn't seem like the kind of thing that would suit a beaver, especially not me so…"

"Aha, hem!" Freddy cleared his throat loudly. "Excuse me, boss. I didn't mean to put you on the spot. If you don't want to tell us what's going on, it's okay. I'm sure you have your reasons, and we all know that you're looking out for us. I mean, it's not like you would ever abandon us or anything. We trust you, Billy, you're our leader, our rock, our foundation, the glue that holds our team togeth…"

"Promotion! They offered me a promotion." Billy interrupted.

The room erupted with excitement,

"Congrats!" cried the cougars.

"Sensational!" said Sonya Sloth.

The cheetahs chimed in. "Cheers!"

"Fantastic!" followed the fish. "Fabulous news."

"No. Not fabulous," Billy replied. "The job is on the other side of the lake. I would have to leave the team."

Fearless Franky Flounder fussed with his fins while fancy Freeda frowned. Fretful Felix feared Fernando would faint and Phil felt famished.

Everyone was happy for Billy. He was a great team leader and they were all sure he would make an excellent executive. But no one wanted to see him go, either. Billy was even more conflicted than the rest of the team.

"Don't worry," he told the group. "Nothing is definite yet. I only agreed to try it out. I'm sure I'll be back in a couple of weeks."

On Saturday afternoon Billy sat in the sun scribbling sets of instructions for his team. The Fabulous Five would fortify the foundation at the Fir Tree dam while the cats collaborated to keep critters contained at Conifer Creek. Of course, Sonya Sloth's secretarial skills would keep everything shipshape on the south shore of the lake. But Billy's brow furrowed in frustration as he pondered his position on what to do with Freddy Fox. Undoubtedly, Freddy would try to convince the others that he was in charge while Billy was away, and he would create tons of problems.

"I know," Billy thought, "I'll take Freddy with me. Then I can keep him out of trouble, and he won't bother the rest of the team."

So, Sunday at sunset they set out to swim across the lake. It was a long journey, and Billy found that Freddy was surprisingly good company. Of course, he was trying to slyly squeeze secret info out of Billy the whole time but still having someone with him made Billy's swim seem shorter.

They arrived on the north shore of the lake just before dawn but already creatures were hustling and bustling about. At first Billy was excited to see so many workers doing so much work, but as he and Freddy made their way to headquarters and the sun began to rise the flurry of activity grew ever faster. As all sorts of creatures on all kinds of work teams scurried this way and that, Billy began to notice the lack of organization in their work. He knew he could make improvements, but there was so much going on. Where could he even start? It was all a little overwhelming.

Just then Benny Bear came by. "Billy! You're right on time. I see you brought Fox with you."

"Yes, sir. I hope you don't mind. I knew there would be a lot to catch up on and I thought Freddy might be able to help me with that."

"I don't mind at all. Anything you need, Billy. You just say the word. Let me show you to your new office, and I'm sure we can have someone find a place for um… Fox there."

As they walked into his new office, Billy could hardly believe his eyes. It was huge. And the view was amazing. Billy could see the whole dam construction site. Although, there were so many files and plans on his desk that he had to stand on his tiptoes to see over them.

"Wow! Benny. I never expected anything like this." Billy blurted.

"Well, you are an executive now, Billy. Besides I thought it would be good for you to be able to see the whole site. There should even be a pair of binoculars in here somewhere. I'll give you some time to get settled in and I'll be back in a few hours to take you to lunch. I hope you like salmon."

In fact, Billy did like salmon, but he rarely ate it. He always felt a bit guilty afterwards, but as long as the Fabulous Five didn't find out he figured it would be fine.

At lunch time Benny took Billy to see the beaver den he had told him about. It was even more impressive than his office. The pups wouldn't have to share a bedroom or a bathroom anymore and there was even room for the grandbeavers to visit. From there they went to Benny's favorite lunch spot and as expected the salmon was delicious.

Back at the office, Billy had been so busy that it was mid-afternoon before he realized that he hadn't seen that sly Freddy Fox since first thing that morning. He decided he would take a walk to explore the HQ and see if he could find Freddy. He found a door with a Post It note on it that said "Freddy Fox," but Freddy wasn't there.

That's odd, Billy thought, it looks more like a broom closet than an office. He finally found Freddy in the employee lounge telling jokes and laughing with a large group of new friends. Freddy, it turned out, had spent his day sucking up to as many new people as he could. He volunteered to pick up lunch three times and had already been to the coffee shop twice. He hadn't done any actual work, but he had learned his way around the neighborhood, and he was already on a first name basis with most of the grizzly bears.

"That Freddy Fox is a fast one," thought Billy. "I just hope I can keep him out of trouble while we're here."

Over the next few days, Billy brushed up on all the details of the project, and Freddy was even somewhat helpful, when he wasn't busy bothering bears. He liked to remind them what a wonderful worker he was.

Billy checked in sometimes with Sonya Sloth on the south shore. As expected, everything was calm as can be. The fabulous five had Fir Tree fit as a fiddle and of course the cats had Conifer Creek covered. He really missed the rest of the team and he was feeling fairly homesick, but he also felt really good about the work he was doing at HQ.

In just a few days he had solved some problems and increased efficiency. The workers were feeling happier than they had in a while and productivity was already taking off. By the end of the week, Billy was feeling more confused than ever.

Around four on Friday, Freddy found his way to Billy's office. "Weekend's almost here, boss," Freddy said in a cheerful tone. "Are you excited for our swim home?"

"I sure am, Freddy. I can't wait to see the wife and pups. I really miss them."

"I bet you do, boss, but just think, your new den is so close to the office, you'll be able to see the family more than ever, after you officially make your promotion permanent, of course."

"It's only been a week, Freddy. I haven't made any decisions yet."

"Are you kidding me? You're doing a great job, boss. The grizzly bears can't stop talking about how amazing you are, even when their mouths are full of fish, which is kind of gross, but they love you. And they gave you that beautiful den and that really awesome office. What in the woods could ever make you say no to a deal like this?"

"You, and the rest of the team."

"I don't understand, boss. We're all really happy for you. Sure, we'll miss you, but you've taught us well. We'll be okay."

"I know you will. In fact, I think I need you guys a lot more than you need me. Don't get me wrong, this new job is great, but we've got a great thing going on the other side of the lake, and I don't want to mess that up either."

"I get it now!" Freddy exclaimed. "I know what your problem is. Boss, you've got binary responsibility."

"Binary responsibility? What in the woods is that? And where did you even learn a word like binary, anyway?"

"I'll have you know sir, that I learned it from Mr. Lawrence Lion with whom I was once acquainted, and it means that your responsibility to the company and your duty to your team are pulling you in two different directions."

"So, what's a guy supposed to do about that?"

"The lion didn't say but I suppose you have to pick one or the other. Unless…"

"Unless what?"

"Never mind. It's too crazy."

"Unless what?" Billy repeated, much more insistently.

"Well, maybe there's a way you can get both responsibilities going the same direction."

All that weekend, Billy pondered his predicament: how could he reconcile his binary responsibilities? How could he come up with one plan that would satisfy both?

First thing Monday morning, Billy went to see Benny Bear. "I have an idea I'd like to run by you, sir."

"Sure thing, Billy. What's on your mind?"

"Well, sir, you've got a lot of good workers on this side of the lake. Some of them may even be as good as my team on the south shore, but to be completely honest with you sir, none of them are better than my team. So here is what I'd like to do. I'd like to rotate different members of my team over to this side of the lake on a weekly basis. That way, they can help me run this project and still ensure that things run smoothly on the south shore. Also, the folks here will benefit by learning from the best team in the woods. What do you think?"

"Like I said, Billy, anything you need. It sounds like you've got all of your responsibilities covered."

Chapter 3

The Theory of Binary Responsibility

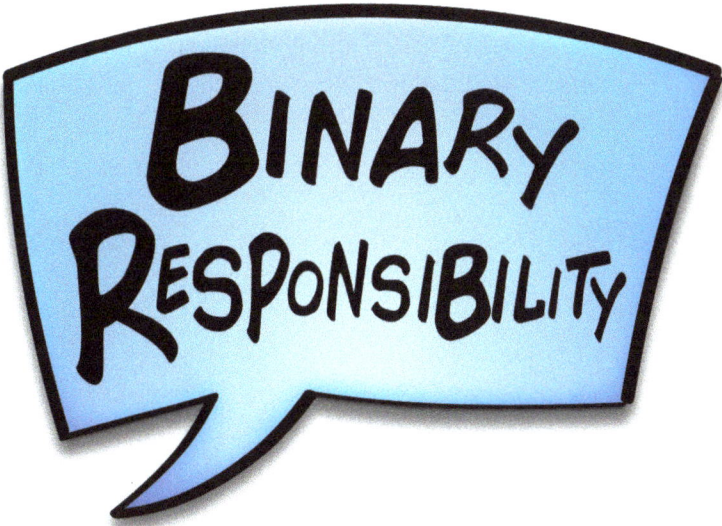

We often have organizational or individual goals and abilities that are not in line with each other. For example, Backwoods Builders needs a new division manager. Franky Fish wants to be a manager like Benny Bear. But becoming a manager would mean not being able to interact in the same way with the other fish and being more individualistic in nature. While Franky wants the pay raise and the title as a goal for his career, his abilities don't match the job. The organization needs a manager in place, or it cannot open that division. As fish feel loyal to the company, Franky takes the job because he feels it's his responsibility to take it. This feeling is called "binary responsibility." When this occurs, the employee can feel literally like a "fish out of water" in the new position and it can create many management issues.

Described by Lawrence
You feel two responsibilities in yourself and you have to pick one or the other: yourself or your company. Responsibility can occur due to loyalty or need (money, benefits, title etc.). No matter the choice, the responsibility will determine your future in the company and your future as a professional.

Section II: Application to Organizational Psychology

Chapter 4

Organizational Psychology and Backwoods Builders

Cristina Cortes
The Chicago School of Professional Psychology
Clinical Forensic Psychology Doctoral Student

Debra Warner, Psy.D.
Forensic Psychologist and Full Professor
The Chicago School of Professional Psychology

Close your eyes and imagine you see a small brown beaver. Think about its long tail and big white buck teeth. Now, imagine this beaver walking up to a fox. The fox has red fur and long pointy ears. Both the beaver and fox make their way over to a bush, where they see a huge brown grizzly bear chatting with a small blue fish. In the not too far distance, a mountain lion and a cheetah are discussing different running styles as they approach a sleepy sloth hanging from a tree. Lastly, imagine a strong lion walking up to the 7 very different animals and talking about the weather.

Now, open your eyes. You may be very confused. You may be thinking, "lions and grizzly bears don't live in the same terrain" or "these animals would never be around each other." Well, you are right on both counts. However, the spirits and attitudes of these animals can be seen among different individuals in a workplace setting. Not everyone will be the same type of animal or have the same type of attitude, but they all must come together to get a job done. Looking at the way people interact with each other in the workplace or in a social organization is organizational psychology.

What is Organizational Psychology?
Carpinteo (2017) explained organizational psychology (OP) as a psychological "specialty that deals with the application of scientific concepts and interpretative models, consisting of devised technological interventions, upon mental and behavioral aspects of manmade organizations with modern societies." Organizational psychology can be referred to as industrial, work, or I-O psychology. Many different organizations make up our society today, including schools, universities, hospitals, and companies like Backwoods Builders.

For this branch of psychology, organization is defined as a "complex entity that contains a plurality of elements or members, forming unity or operating as a certain whole that endeavors to reach goals or ends, which represent the basic reason for its existence" (Carpinteo, 2017). Within an organization, certain elements are present, including leadership staff, rank-and-file employees, communication between the two groups, and the mutual goals that both groups need to accomplish. For example, the Lions needed leadership (Billy Beaver) to build a dam and Billy Beaver wanted to build the dam with his team. Both had a goal to be accomplished.

The Employees and Leadership
All employees are as essential as the CEO. They are among the most integral parts of an organization. The staff can have

different attitudes and styles. Are they zoned in like the fox? Strong and silent like the lion? Each staff member will additionally have different management styles, including transformational, authentic, or proactive vitality management.

Yavuz (2020) explains transformational leadership as "developing the purpose of performing leadership roles of followers." This type of leader wants their employees to be just as creative as themselves. Transformational leaders stimulate and help their employees with their creative process (Yavuz, 2020). On the other hand, authentic leadership focuses on and develops the inner self (Yavuz, 2020). Authentic leaders "provide durable relationships and lead with purpose, meaning and values" (Avolio & Gardner, 2005, p.329). Whatever the leadership style, employees will have a connection to how they feel regarding their performance in the organization.

Benny Bear allowed Billy Beaver to cover all his responsibilities in his own style of leadership. This allowed Billy Beaver to stimulate his creative narrative process, fulfill his needs, and utilize the strengths of his team.

Proactive vitality management is a "specific form of proactive behavior aimed at oneself by improving one's own physical and psychological state" (Bakker, Petrou, Op den Kamp, & Tims, 2020). In this type of management, the staff changes parts of themselves to change their future (Bakker, Petrou, Opden Kamp, & Tims, 2020). These staff members "engage in this behavior when they think they can perform the behavior that is needed ("can-do motivation"), have a reason to behave in a proactive way ("reason to motivation"), and feel they have the resources to engage in the behavior ("energized to motivation") (Bakker, Petrou, Op den Kamp, & Tims, 2020).

Sonya Sloth may be slow moving but her work is done well. In an organization, creating an environment creates a space for people's strengths and weaknesses and allows for an employee to produce pro-work behaviors that match abilities to create internal satisfaction. If managers try and create an environment that goes against Sonya Sloth's natural state (i.e. working faster), it may create a negative state for her physically as she cannot move quickly, thereby affecting her psychological state of being. Leaders who keep proactive vitality in mind can help ensure employee satisfaction and productivity.

Having a group of employees working together in harmony is ideal, just like the animals at the beginning of the story. This may not always be perfect, but it can happen when the right mindset is established, and the employees feel comfortable. Think about what kind of employee you are or want to be. Are you a beaver, lion, fox, or a grizzly bear? Just like the animals, each employee has different gifts that make them essential. One may be better at organization, where another may be better at interacting with people. Employees may not know their abilities at first but can develop them through the years and with the right organizational support, have greater employee satisfaction.

Employee Satisfaction

Dugguh and Dennis (2014) explained that job satisfaction refers to the "attributes and feelings people have about their work." Several features can influence the way an employee feels about their job. This includes attitude towards pay, working conditions, co-workers and managers, career prospects and intrinsic aspects of the job (Dugguh and Dennis, 2014).

Two-factor theory comprises two factors: intrinsic or motivator factors, "work itself, responsibilities, and achievements" (Anderson, 2001) and extrinsic or hygiene factors, "company policies, working conditions, and pay" (Anderson, 2001). Research has found that intrinsic factors were "more strongly correlated with satisfaction, while extrinsic factors were more strongly correlated with dissatisfaction" (Anderson, 2001). With this being said, jobs should focus on motivator factors, so their employees are more likely to stay and be satisfied in their position.

Franky Fox is someone who may not have satisfaction in his role. He may have other traits that are not fitting his job duties, which is why he tries to sabotage others and aligns himself with Billy Beaver's success. The story tells us that Franky has been placed in the woodshed. He likely is not stimulated or does not feel his talents are utilized. He may have also been placed in the woodshed to distance him from other employees, however the trait that placed him there is part of his character. He may have an unmet need for planning that has not been cultivated and the need is manifesting in inappropriate ways. A good leader will cultivate that need to create an environment to utilize Freddy Fox's traits as a strength. That strength will aid in job satisfaction for Freddy Fox and decrease turnover.

Turnover

Anderson (2001) identified turnover as a withdrawal behavior. There are several definitions as to what turnover truly is, but it can be looked at as the employee's movement in an organization or social system (Anderson, 2001). Turnover can be correlated to the employee's job satisfaction. Research has shown that the "potential for alternative employment or perceptions thereof, condition the impact of satisfaction on quitting" (Anderson, 2001).

This subject is complicated by the fact that each employee is different, and therefore will react to different stimuli. However, there are basic factors that are relevant for each person. Treating employees with respect, kindness, and dignity will make them want to stay at a company.

Chandler, Chelsea, and Chuck Cheetah do not want Billy Beaver to get the promotion because Billy Beaver is set in his ways and does not believe in going home early. Their intrinsic needs of being home outweighs the organizational needs. For Billy to be successful he would have realize that his views on work and business differ from Chandler, Chelsea, and Chuck Cheetah and must recognize their intrinsic needs to be at home while motivating them to be as productive as they can while at work.

Chapter 5

Summary

All animals can have traits of others. People in organizations often do, but people are easier to manage when they conform with one or the other. However, we are made up of differences. This book expresses the importance of allowing your employees to be who they are in your organization. It illustrates how problematic it can be for employees to strive to meet expectations that they do not feel make them meet their full potential. While we can train and mentor employees to become effective, we also have to balance their job satisfaction and the satisfaction of those around them and those who support them.

About the Authors

Lawrence Carey
Lawrence is a fourth-grade student who enjoys math and science. His dream is to become a paleontologist. However, for right now he settles for being a human Marvel Comics encyclopedia and playing with his faithful dog Orion, "the force puppy."

Debra Warner, Psy.D. (Mama)
Dr. Debra Warner is a Full Professor in the Forensic Psychology department of The Chicago School of Professional Psychology Los Angeles. Her areas of expertise include: male survivors of trauma and violence, community gang intervention, immigration and mental health, competency, psychological testing, diversity, personality disorders, and substance abuse. Dr. Warner is a TEDx and invited speaker. She has been a quoted expert in books, television and radio.

Appendix of Animal Facts

Beavers, Foxes and Grizzly Bears

Jessica Torres
The Chicago School of Professional Psychology
Clinical Forensic Psychology Doctoral Student

The wildlife kingdom includes mammals, reptiles, birds, fish, insects, mollusks, amphibians, and crustaceans (Morris, 2002). There are different types of mammals that live all around the world, human beings and animals. Mammals have hair or fur on their body to help keep them warm (Morris, 2002). Baby mammals are fed with milk that is produced by the body of their mother (Morris, 2002). They also live in different places: land or water, or in different climates: freezing, temperate or hot. Beavers, lions, foxes, and grizzly bears are all considered mammals.

Beavers

Beavers are considered members of the rodent family of animals and their average length is between 41-67 inches (DK Pub, 2006). They are quite large in size, not similar to a typical sized rodent. They belong to the Castoridae family and have a lifespan of 13-20 years (DK Pub, 2006). Their habitat includes rivers, streams, and lakes (DK Pub, 2006). Beavers are known to have originated in North America and Northern Eurasia (DK Pub, 2006). The typical number of babies a mother beaver gives birth to is 2-4. Their food intake consists of buds, water plants, leaves, and roots and inner barks of trees (DK Pub, 2006). They live in water and are well known for their dam building skills.

The American beaver has a flat tail, wood chopping teeth, sleek body meant for swimming, and thick fur (DK

Pub, 2006). A beaver's flat tail helps control both their steering and speed while they are swimming. Their gnawing teeth are extremely large and have the potential to cut down a tree that is up to 39 inches wide (DK Pub, 2006). They have two large teeth on both lower and upper jaws, located in the front of the mouth. Beavers' teeth continue to grow and do not wear down because they are sharp (DK Pub, 2006). Their jaw muscle is very strong and is used to cut down trees and branches at a fast speed. From that tree, they build dams using their engineering skills. Their thick fur, which is waterproof, keeps them warm in and out of the water (DK Pub, 2006).

These animal engineers live and work in tiny family groups (DK Pub, 2006). They are active animals throughout the day and work together as a family to build their dams and lodges. They work by cutting through trees and branches and swim together by holding them in their mouths. Beavers are very cautious and protective of their family members. If they sense danger or see a predator, they signal each other by slapping their powerful flat tails on the water as a warning to swim for safety (DK Pub, 2006). Their dam homes are built with branches, mud, and stones. These tools stop the flow of water and form a deep pond. Once they have built their home, they use it to shelter from the cold weather and as protection from other animals (DK Pub, 2006).

Foxes

Foxes belong to the Canidae family group along with wolves and other meat eaters. They originated from Europe, Asia, North and South America, and Africa (DK Pub, 2006). Their lifespan averages 6 years and their size ranges from 35-59 inches in length (DK Pub, 2006). A fox's preferred habit is grasslands, deserts, and woodlands (DK Pub, 2006). Their food consumption consists of insects, dead animals, fruit, birds, and small mammals (DK Pub, 2006). They have narrow pointed faces and long bushy tails.

There is a total of 21 different types of foxes around the world (DK Pub, 2006). Since foxes are considered foragers, they tend to eat anything they are able to find and they have the ability to travel far while looking for food, without getting tired (DK Pub, 2006). During their hunting process, they travel alone but live in small family groups.

The purpose of a red fox's long bushy tail is to help balance themselves while they hunt their prey (DK Pub, 2006). Foxes have long, strong legs that allow them to move fast during long distance travels. They have excellent sight, hearing, and smell. This is the reason for their big eyes, nose, and ears (DK Pub, 2006). Foxs' front paws become stretched out and ready to make a landing to squish their prey while they are hunting. They can leap up to 3 feet straight into the air (DK Pub, 2006). They are known to be very intelligent hunters due to their high level of alertness for danger and prey (DK Pub, 2006). A fox's thick fur allows them to survive cold temperature as low as -58 degrees (DK Pub, 2006). Fox prints are considered toepad prints and they have hair between each pad, which may blur the print from prey or humans (DK Pub, 2006).

Grizzly Bears

Bears are large and strong mammals that are primarily meat eaters but will eat nearly anything they come across. They belong to the Ursidae family of animals and have a lifespan of 25-30 years (DK Pub, 2006). They have poor eyesight and depend highly on their sense of smell. They originated in Asia, Europe, North and South America (DK Pub, 2006). Their typical habitat consists of grasslands, forests, and mountains (DK Pub, 2006).

Their diet includes fruits, insects, fish, small animals, roots, and dead animals (DK Pub, 2006). Bears may grow to be extremely large and their size may vary between 3-9 feet long. They also have strong bodies, strong legs, and lots of fur. Their heads are quite large due to their strong jaws and teeth, which are used to crush the wide variety of foods they eat. Their large snouts allow them to smell food since their eyesight and hearing is poor (DK Pub, 2006).

Grizzly bears are brown and have white tips on their hair, known as grizzled hair (DK Pub, 2006). They specifically live in the woodlands and meadows in the northwest of North America (DK Pub, 2006). The soles of their feet are furry, and they take small steps, hardly lifting their paws from the ground (DK Pub, 2006). Their sharp curved claws enable them to dig up food and to attack. They also enable them to climb trees in search for food. Bears consume meat, berries, and insects during the fall to increase their fat reserves as preparation of sleeping in their dens during the cold winter weather (DK Pub, 2006). During the summer they move toward streams to catch fish, such as salmon.

They also walk around on all fours while chasing prey and are able to run fast over a short distance (DK Pub, 2006). When they are hunting prey, they stand on their hind legs in attempt to make themselves look much bigger, scarier, and to scope out a larger amount of their environment (DK Pub, 2006). When standing on both their hind legs, grizzly bears may stand 10 feet tall. They tend to open their mouths to display their big teeth to their prey (DK Pub, 2006).

Oh, and Cheetahs, Fish and Sloths

Gabriella Pacheco, M.A.
The Chicago School of Professional Psychology
Clinical Forensic Psychology Doctoral Student

Cheetahs

While most people know that cheetahs are found in Africa, there is a small population that can also be found in Iran (National Geographic Kids, 2019). Cheetahs are the fastest land animal in the world, able to go from 0-60 mph in just 3 seconds. Although they have a lot of energy to run and catch their prey, their energy only lasts so long, making their run less than a minute before slowing down.

Cheetahs normally eat rabbits, gazelles and warthogs but they will eat whatever animal they are able to catch (National Geographic Kids, 2019). While lions and tigers tend to hunt in the evening hours to surprise their prey, cheetahs tend to hunt in the daytime, so they do not have to compete with those other predators. Hunting during the day gives the cheetah the advantage since they have first access to the prey. If they were to wait until evening, the bigger and stronger animals such as lions could take up all the food which would leave the cheetah starving. Cheetahs only need to drink water once every 3 to 4 days, which is convenient since the African deserts are dry.

Cheetahs can mostly be found in groups as they are social animals. They also tend to hunt together. Female cheetahs tend to have around 3 cubs that live with them for up to 2 years, so they learn hunting techniques (Sartore, 2018). The average life span of a cheetah is about 10-12 years. Sadly, there are only an estimated 9,000-12,000 cheetahs left in Africa due to being hunted by humans for sport and trophies. Cheetahs are the only big cats that cannot roar (Sartore, 2018).

Fish

Fish have been around for more than 500 million years (NOAA Fisheries, 2019). You can actually find out how old a fish is by looking at the rings on its scales, although each fish is different so the rings could also be located in other places. According to National Geographic (2012), all fish share the same two traits" they live in water and are vertebrates. There are over 20,000 species of fish and that is because the Earth is 70% water.

They live in all types of water: including oceans, rivers, and lakes. Most fish lay eggs, however some, like the shark, give birth to their live young. Most fish tend to stay together in what is called a school so they can appear bigger to scare off predators. Some fish also camouflage themselves within the sea plants to hide from predators.

Fish are able to detect movement in the water through the sounds, chemicals and electrical impulses that water conducts (National Geographic, 2012). When fish are not traveling, they tend to rest. They do not sleep like humans, however. They must remain on high alert for predators with their brains and bodies awake. Fish rest by simply reducing their energy use before swimming again (U.S. Department of Commerce, & National Oceanic and Atmospheric Administration, 2014). Since each species of fish is different, it is difficult to say exactly how long fish live. Some fish live for a few weeks and other species can live for over 20 years. According to NOAA Fisheries (2019), the smallest fish is the tiny goby and the largest fish is the whale shark. This shows the variety of fish that are out there.

Sloths

Sloths have been around for many thousands of years. Back then, they could grow to be as large as an elephant. (Bradford, 2018). While indigenous to Central and South America, they can be found in zoos and animal conservation all over the United States.

Sloths may look the same, however there are two different types: the two-toed sloth and the three-toed sloth. However, the names are misleading since they really refer to the number of claws on their front paws (A-Z Animals, 2020).

While their claws are used to climb up and down trees, the claws also protect them from enemies such as jaguars, snakes and humans. It takes a sloth about a minute just to climb 1 foot.

Sloths spend most of their lives in trees and only come down from the tree once a week to poop. Their lives revolve around sleeping and eating. They sleep around 15 hours a day and eat leaves and occasionally insects. If they are desperate, sloths will eat small reptiles and small birds (A-Z Animals, 2020).

Sloths need to be careful since they can actually starve to death on a full stomach. According to The Sloth Conservation Foundation (2020) a microbe in their stomach can die if their body gets too cold, which makes it impossible for the digestion process to finish.

Sloths are technically blind when it is too bright outside due to a condition called "rod monochromacy," which essentially is a lack of cones in the eyes (The Sloth Conservation Foundation, 2020). Although sloths are extremely slow, they love to swim and are quite fast in the water. This helps them survive in the rainforest when there is flooding.

Interestingly, according to Lax (2019), sloths have a symbiotic relationship with algae. Algae grows on their fur which protects the sloth and the sloth provides shelter for the algae. It is unknown exactly how long sloths live in the wild but in captivity, they have been found to live up to 30 years.

And a Few More Too!

Allison Roddy
The Chicago School of Professional Psychology
Clinical Forensic Psychology Doctoral Student

Cougars

What is the difference between cougars, mountain lions, panthers, pumas, and catamounts? None! According to National Geographic (2015), cougars, mountain lions, panthers, pumas, and catamounts all belong to the small cat family. Unlike lions, tigers, or leopards, cougars do not roar but rather purr, similar to a house cat (Nature Mapping, 2011). Cougars also use low-pitched growls, hisses, and yowls to communicate to other cougars in certain circumstances (Animal Diversity Web, 2003). They have long bodies and smaller heads with round ears (Nature Mapping, 2011). The cougar's fur can be grey or reddish tan with white patches on their muzzles and chest, and black markings on their faces, ears, and tails (Nature Mapping, 2011).

Although cougars are in the small cat family, they are considered the largest cat in the category. Cougars can vary in size, with a length from nose to tail between 6 to 8 feet (Cougar Network, 2015). They can weigh between 75 and 250 pounds, with females weighing around 120 pounds (Animal Diversity Web, 2003). Their paws have sharp claws that can be hidden while walking, but when needed for catching prey, they can be deadly (Nature Mapping, 2011). Their claws also come in handy when they need to climb trees, as they can jump up to 18 feet and utilize trees to target their prey (Cougar Network, 2015).

Cougars are carnivores and their diets consist of a variety of animals (Cougar Network, 2015). Because of their quiet stalking, excellent vision, and jumping skills, cougars

Carey & Warner   52 are able to prey upon animals much larger than themselves, such as moose, but they also consume elk, deer, caribou, coyotes, bobcats and smaller animals like squirrels, porcupines, and even fish (Animal Diversity Web, 2003).

Cougars are the most widespread land mammals in the Western Hemisphere, ranging all over North and South America (Nature Mapping, 2011). This is due to cougars being habitat generalists, which means they are able to survive in different areas from the desert to forest (Cougar Network, 2015).

Cougar cubs remain reliant on their mothers until they learn to hunt and roam on their own, which occurs around 12 months old (Animal Diversity Web, 2003). Once big enough, cougars tend to live on their own (Nature Mapping, 2011).

Lions

Lions are a symbol of strength, courage, and power, and that is shown in their roar, which can be heard up to 5 miles away (World Wildlife Foundation, 2011). Lions are part of the big cat family and are second in size to tigers (National Geographic, 2015).

According to the Smithsonian's National Zoo and Conservation Biology Institute (2018), the bodies of lions and tigers are so similar, that without their coats, only experts can tell them apart. When standing, lions can range in size from 4.5 to 6.5 feet tall, weighing up to 420 pounds (National Geographic, 2015). The fur of a lion is yellowish-gold, though males have shaggy manes that can range in color with blond, yellowish-god, and black (Smithsonian's National Zoo and Conservation Biology Institute, 2018).

Lions were once seen all over Africa and parts of Asia and Europe, but unfortunately, 94% of their range has been diminished (National Geographic, 2015). Today, lions are considered a vulnerable population, only being found in the wild of Africa (Smithsonian's National Zoo and Conservation Biology Institute, 2018). Their population vulnerability is due to a lack of prey, but also due to human trophy hunting (National Geographic, 2015). Like other cats, lions can survive in many different habitats, though they prefer areas where they can easily hunt prey, such as grassland, open woodland, and dense scrub (National Geographic, 2015).

Lions are the world's most social cats, as they are the only cats that live in groups, which are called prides (National Geographic, 2015). Prides may contain up to 40 lions, with the majority females. Although mother lions are very protective and caring of their cubs, female lions are the hunters for the pride (World Wildlife Foundation, 2011). The male lions defend the pride's territory from intruders and do so by claiming dominance while roaring (Smithsonian's National Zoo and Conservation Biology Institute, 2018).

Male lions have manes to make them look bigger and scarier to their prey. Their mane also protects their neck and back from being bitten or clawed during a fight with an enemy (DK Pub, 2006). Occasionally, male lions in the same pride challenge each other to claim their dominance in the group (Morris, 2002). Male lions are slower than lionesses, and their larger size makes them easily spotted by enemies. In their group, male lions eat prior to the rest of the pride.

Lions tend to prey on large animals such as zebras, antelopes, and wildebeests (National Geographic, 2015). Since their prey can outrun them, lions tend to hunt in teams and stalk their prey (World Wildlife Foundation, 2011). Did you know lions can leap as far as 36 feet? (World Wildlife Foundation, 2011).

References

Anderson, N. (2005). *Handbook of industrial, work and organizational psychology* (Vol. 1, Personnel Psychology). SAGE Publications.

Anderson, N. (2001). *Handbook of industrial, work and organizational psychology* (Vol. 2, Organizational Psychology). SAGE Publications.

Animal Diversity Web. (2003). *Cougar.* Retrieved from https://animaldiversity.org/site/accounts/information/Puma_concolor.html

Avolio, B. J., & Gardner, W. L. (2005). Authentic leadership development: Getting to the root of positive forms of leadership. *The Leadership Quarterly*, 16(3), 315–338 doi:10.1016/j.leaqua.2005.03.001.

A-Z Animals. (2020, January 21). *Sloth.* Retrieved from https://a-z-animals.com/animals/sloth/

Bakker, A. B., Petrou, P., Op den Kamp, E. M., & Tims, M. (2020). Proactive vitality management, work engagement, and creativity: The role of goal orientation. *Applied Psychology*, 69(2), 351-378.

Bradford, A. (2018, November 26). *Sloths: The world's slowest mammals*. Retrieved from https://www.livescience.com/27612-sloths.html

Cougar Network. (2015). *Cougar facts*. Retrieved from https://www.cougarnet.org/facts

Dorling Kindersley animal encyclopedia. (2006). DK Pub. New York, NY.

Dugguh, S. I., & Dennis, A. (2014). Job satisfaction theories: Traceability to employee performance in organizations. *IOSR Journal of Business and Management*, 16(5), 11-18.

Lax, A. (2019, July 22). *10 facts about sloths, nature's slowest animals*. Retrieved from

https://www.worldanimalprotection.us/news/10-
facts-about-sloths-natures-slowest-animals

Maps, N. G. (2019, June 14).
Mountain lion. Retrieved from
https://kids.nationalgeographic.com/animals/mamm
als/mountain-lion/

Morris, N. (2002). *Children's first encyclopedia*. Parragon.

National Geographic. (2012). *Fish*. Retrieved from
https://www.nationalgeographic.com/animals/fish/

National Geographic. (2015). *African lions*. Retrieved from
https://www.nationalgeographic.com/animals/mam
mals/a/african-lion/

National Geographic Kids. (2019, October 31). *10 top
cheetah facts!* Retrieved from
https://www.natgeokids.com/nz/discover/animals/ge
neral-animals/cheetah-facts/

National Park Service. (2015, February 28).

Nature Mapping. (2011). *Animal facts: Cougar*. Retrieved
from
http://naturemappingfoundation.org/natmap/facts/co
ugar_712.html

NOAA Fisheries. (2019, September 13). *Fun facts about
fascinating fish*. Retrieved from
https://www.fisheries.noaa.gov/national/outreach-
and-education/fun-facts-about-fascinating-fish

Sartore, J. (2018, September 17). *Cheetah*. Retrieved from
https://www.nationalgeographic.com/animals/mam
mals/c/cheetah/

Shersby, M. (n.d.). *10 amazing cougar facts you need to
know*. Retrieved from
https://www.discoverwildlife.com/animal-
facts/mammals/facts-about-cougars/

The Sloth Conservation Foundation. (2020, February 22). *10 incredible facts about the sloth*. Retrieved from https://slothconservation.com/10-incredible-facts-about-the-sloth/?gclid=EAIaIQobChMIl_p19fD6AIVksBkCh 3LiAKWEAAYASAAEgKK4fD_BwE

Smithsonian's National Zoo and Conservation Biology Institute. (2018). *Lion.* Retrieved   from https://nationalzoo.si.edu/animals/lion

U.S. Department of Commerce & National Oceanic and Atmospheric Administration. (2014, September 15). Do fish sleep? Retrieved from https://oceanservice.noaa.gov/facts/fish-sleep.html

World Wildlife Foundation. (2011). *Ten interesting facts about lions.* Retrieved from https://www.worldwildlife.org/blogs/good-nature-travel/posts/ten-interesting-facts-about-lions

Yavuz, M. (2020). Transformational leadership and authentic leadership as practical implications of positive organizational psychology. In *Handbook of Research on Positive Organizational Behavior for Improved Workplace Performance* (pp. 122-139). IGI Global.